CW00764831

FINISHING LINE PRESS
www.finishinglinepress.com

Silence coming up for air

poems by

Ruby Turok-Squire

Finishing Line Press
Georgetown, Kentucky

Silence coming up for air

ISBN 978-1-63534-156-0 First Edition

ACKNOWLEDGMENTS

I am grateful to the editors of the following publications in which some of these poems first appeared:

The Antigonish Review (Canada): "The Phantom Fundamental", "Progression" and "The Harp Strings";
Canadian Literature: "The Piano Strings";
The Fortnightly Review (UK): "Partita for Solo Violin";
Fugue: A Journal of Contemporary Literature: "Preludes for Solo Piano"

Publisher: Leah Maines

Editor: Christen Kincaid

Cover Art: Jenny Bloomfield, Grey Black Shift (detail) 2016

Cover Design: Elizabeth Maines McCleavy

Printed in the USA on acid-free paper.
Order online: www.finishinglinepress.com
also available on amazon.com

Author inquiries and mail orders:
Finishing Line Press
P. O. Box 1626
Georgetown, Kentucky 40324
U. S. A.

Table of Contents

Preludes for Solo Piano........ 1

The Piano Strings........ 7

The Pitches........ 8

The Phantom Fundamental........ 12

Partita for Solo Violin........ 13

The Intervals........ 18

Improvisation in 4/4........ 23

Progression........ 25

The Harp Strings........ 27

Glossary........ 28

Aria........ 31

For Lynn Powell—
as they have always been.

In loving memory of
Peggy Squire

Preludes for Solo Piano

I

What I have wanted for so long
is to begin,
by which I mean, to have no memory.

To press a key down and listen and let it die.

To press a key down and listen and let it die.

To look up and see
every feather

waiting for the direction of gravity
to be declared.

II

I find I am standing
in the middle of a long flat maze with black

walls and white floors.

How unnatural
it is, to stand still in a maze.
I let out

a melody for a
thread

behind me.

III

My fingers are falling to the keys
as if to the earth—

their earth,
an earth that falls
away under them and rises as they rise.

By the sound, I could
believe the earth had sunk

into me
slightly, and is emerging.

IV

Since air is the ground you walk on,
music, what do you breathe?

I have noticed you grow
best when I close
my eyes, that darkness is your light.

My ears breathe in the sound you send:

they are grateful. In exchange,
I give out more time. You inhale it
hungrily and it colours you.

V

Hands that were mine
having other limbs to end—

limbs that are lines of sound,
moving without desire

to add to anything—
if I am silent then,
it is because I am singing,

singing about how
my mouth was an illusion.

VI

There is a silence after the end
when I raise my hands, having done
all I can, and all of you

wait; a silence that lasts as long as the forearms
remain tense;
each time, I tell myself, this time

I will hold the silence
forever, this time
I will not give you your lives back.

The Piano Strings

Once, you lifted the long roof
and bent your head
close to us; there was no notation for this.

Our stillness—stillness,
which was movement gone silent—made us
seem to listen, and so you sang to us

out loud—sang
into us, and we shook,
which made us ring, as though with sympathy.

One ringing noise
answered all your vowels.
You could be reminded of indifference.

Or the beautiful echo could be a beautiful echo.

The Pitches

C

Before you is a palette
on which twelve colours have hardened.

How to wet and mix them
is up to you;
they come alive where their skin flows.

C#

Each note is like a stem
cell of music,
waiting for an organ to learn—

I listen, which is my way of saying,
I accompany them with my heartbeat.

D

Who weaves
this length that disappears as

it is made—
slipping from her fingers, repelling
perfectly the air-beams—

E*b*

Pillar, which as soon as lands
in a voice,
crumbles;

we have the time in our lungs
to walk among these widening ruins.

E

Sharper than the others
to me, slides
through these ears as though both ways,

as though smaller
than the mind's pores.

F

Again, the hand folds in its wings,
plummets into the open

spine
of a string and touches
sound. Touch is sound.

F#

Before you ask where
I find the warmth in this note,

wrap me in it—I will stray
later out into myself
than I could alone.

G

Seconds are the rocks
the scale rushes over,
smoothing.

Still, time is not comforted,
its yells are those of a constant newborn.

G#

Since birth, my ears have been pressed
to the air, waiting
to understand those who speak

behind its walls
these words of pure frequency.

A

Equator of music,
along which we line up our instruments.

Something about being in tune is truthful,
is like reaching nothing
over or under one another.

B*b*

Look, out there, far out
on the silence—

enlarging—which translates
to loudening—then raising its black
sail—

B

If formed in the still
lake of a mouth,
a whole series of notes starts floating

above the lowest; they will go as high as you can hear,
the sourceless reflections.

The Phantom Fundamental

I don't know what made you, only
that you played me a chord
unlike any I could name, while I
stood over you and watched.

As you held down those notes,
I became aware I could hear
a sound like another piano key,
far below the ones you touched.

It was a sound, in fact, too low
to have been made by a piano.
But I could hear it—as silence
collected into itself the far

edges of the resonance, you
lifted your hands and pressed
them down again, and there,
fading in time with the others

was the same, much lower
note we could not explain
hearing, that was as loud to us
as every other in the chord;

louder, even, being, as we
were somewhere beginning to
sense, one that our minds
alone were singing.

Partita for Solo Violin

I. *Allemande*

Sound, I know you live
on silence—when you open
your own lips and let go
of the air, it is what rushes out.

Let me pull it back into your lungs
along my bow, until
I can see you again, with these
eyes I cannot close.

II. *Courante*

I have arrived at a string.
I bend it; it opens.
A new ground

grows up around me,
as if all the sides of my skin were feet—
I run out there.

Four rivers line this ground,
running rapidly uphill.
I must sing a map

to the ear inside my head,
until my fingers hear where to find
each molecule of the water.

Overhead,
a long thin sun
strokes back and forth.

III. *Sarabande*

Here, so carefully,
I almost think time
is what I am pulling

into being—
time, a form of air
I have not yet seen through—

violin, why must we look
over my shoulder—
not the whole way, not enough

to invite the past in,
but enough to stand it on the threshold
of my ears, wanting an answer?

IV. *Gigue*

When the flickering transfers to the fingers
the eyes
go out, go out of their small rooms
into backgrounds beyond mine—

if I open them then,
coming towards me are four
flesh-coloured ants,
recognising their own paths.

What are we building, with this saw
that performs the action of cutting
as if that is enough,
as if nothing has to break?

Hand it to me again, I will not believe
it is one length—
too often has it never ended,
or disappeared at once.

V. *Chaconne*

As the arms breathe,
the dark inside
this wooden shell

begins to do other than grow light.
Once carved,
centuries became the soil

through which its tone reached
deeper, wider:
what happens when the dead age.

Low notes push on my chest;
they ring there, saying
we are who you are.

I, I am the fifth string,
tied here at my neck.
Music presses its fingers into me;

I lean into a passing
note, away
from where it went, circling

the spine's rod
in a slow wind
I do not feel on my skin.

The Intervals

Octave

A mirror is looking
at itself in a mirror.

Between them, sound
throws and catches and throws itself.

Absence meeting absence,
and letting out this noise.

Major Seventh

One drop of paint
has fallen

into a jar of clean water;
listen,

its spiral is making everywhere
blur.

Minor Seventh

A sound so dense
you float in it,

its endless arms
under your arms;

no need to think
here, to move.

Major Sixth

All but the rim
of the chord has eroded: look through.

There is an end to its contents—
to lift

them, slide your hands
under the air.

Minor Sixth

This sound has the darkness
of a tower;

below you, there seems to be a light,
a way out;

you climb down and down,
deaf to the shouts of Escher.

Perfect Fifth

If you could send your eyes
out along these two

lines you are hearing,
it would be

like looking straight ahead,
with the feeling of looking up.

Tritone

A sound is spinning around a point
so fast it seems to multiply.

You hold it to your ears;
however long you wish for

home, it will not settle
on a North.

Perfect Fourth

Space has broken
in two places:

its blood
is flowing

out through these
tooth-marks.

Major Third

Even when you are closest
to smiling,

music, I see
the way your mouth opens like an eye

full of the most
unclearable water.

Minor Third

A river is falling
over rocks, one side of the water folding over

the other, turning
white then clear and white and clear and escaping

like a child trying to catch
its own hand.

Major Second

To play it on the piano
is to feel two

logs sinking
under the flames of the fingers;

later, the season of the pink flowers
and the grey soil.

Minor Second

Moment a knife
makes contact

elongated in the ears, white
of a new split

made endless
before the alarm, the rush.

Perfect Unison

There is a world
built on a single place.

You are the place
and you are standing there.

Around you, the horizon
has curled into a sphere.

Improvisation in 4/4

I come down from my head—
something is appearing in the distance
I need to see closer—
and lean out over my fingers.
I step off the end
of a finger—my foot is converted to a note.
The note has too much weight
on it—I waver—it cannot hold me
for long—then set
another note down into music.
Now the two have each other
to agree they are here, it will become harder
to stay lost—
and that, I realise, is what I want
from this path. Forwards
a few notes, with the assurance of one
who is returning
to a home she has never lived in.
However far I walk,
I have only taken four steps.
My mind keeps ending
at four and beginning again
at one. There is no zero, and five
is another word for one.
How comforting, to have subtracted
everything not whole
from the world, and to find I am left,
counting just the numbers.
Listen, the ground is learning to walk—
I let it out of my feet,
so it can discover its own—
the ground seems to want to walk
across itself and away into the air.

Thought is not the rope
I balance on, it is what I try not to fall
towards, as these hands are
pulled under the rise
and fall of the phrase—it is the one
who breathes now.
Do not help me, I am in pain—
in that there is no space
in me to stop making these sounds—
but a pain without
the presence of any red.

Progression

after J.S. Bach

I *Tonic*

The moment it passes
through us, this chord
has always been our home;
on every side it looks out over leaving.

VI *Relative Minor*

Close one eye then the other and the universe
leaps an inch to the
left;
so the chord changes

IV *Subdominant*

again and here feels harder
to trust;
to hold on, the notes louden
almost into material, then

V *Dominant*

cut down—a clearing in time—
remember how soon we can
have come nowhere,
nowhere is two notes away.

VII°7 *Diminished Seventh*

Through one earth,
if two axes
ran, so is the sound
turning

V7 *Dominant Seventh*

on itself, and turning
around you and inside you
into one
place, through which the sound is leading

II *Supertonic*

you further
from your understanding,
as if that too were an emotion
in need of being voiced in order to end.

V7 *Dominant Seventh*

Higher up, the clouds white
against the dark blue of the fading day;
lower, the clouds grey
against the light blue of the fading day.

I *Tonic*

For a time afterwards, the sky
looks like its own source of light;
there is no brighter part,
it starts everywhere,
a halo without a head.

The Harp Strings

How long you had forgotten us was how much lower we sounded
when you returned, lifted the velvet cover and brushed
your fingers through a scale only unattended time could create.

We had, you could hear, all fallen loose by different amounts,
though nothing else had varied, not our material or place.
In answer, you took out a hollow key, fitted it over the nail

the lowest was wound on, and one by one made your way up the arc,
turning as you went, as delicately as the shape of key allowed,
testing with your free hand the octaves against one another

until they blended and were even, as was required by your music.
Now trying fifths, thirds—the seriousness of the corrections
diminishing—
then one of us tightened, with a shift of the wrist or give of the metal

too far, so that a voice became higher than it knew
how to be, and quickly, while this could still be returned from,
letting the string back out, the wanting to break fading.

Glossary

Accelerando

All fires catch slowly,
but when they do,
all there is
is to watch, dream.

Beating

The place two pitches touch
is a rhythm,
the way the reflection of a bridge
writhes.

Coda

In time,
even the longest
lived of the silences
must come up for air.

Fermata

Arrive at no walls,
no sky:
garden on all six sides.
Lie down there.

Mute

Stop the part of yourself
that would travel to me,
but still
reach me.

Pianissimo

Meaning, let enough escape
for your breath
to stand
dark against your face.

Piano

It can start to feel like the blood
echoing,
as it is for the brain,
the brain, whose soles the blood kisses.

Rubato

Give some of later
to now,
so that if you stepped far back from time,
it would look the same.

Tenuto

Some kinds of the earth need you
to place your whole weight
there without ever
being held.

Timbre

Find the hands to run over my voice,
this is what you will feel; hold a glass jar down
over my voice, until
it drips off the walls, this is what you will taste.

Trill

As a smooth cross,
wherever the sky
lets go,
turns back into wings.

Tutti

Measure the height of our sound
by its shadow;
we built it the way we could:
the way we could not again.

Aria

There is a place I look out over with my voice—

I who have chosen to hide
behind nothing,
to be my own instrument.

The air is the land of that place,
and the sea, and the air,

and the only living being

is my voice,
which moves forever

away from itself
over the land,

and if it should pause, ceases to live.

But when I have breathed
in, it begins
again to hold

together the expanding
edge of its world,

where it always imagines
a part of you,

listener, is
already able to hear

it is your voice.

CPSIA information can be obtained
at www.ICGtesting.com
Printed in the USA
BVHW031025131221
623912BV00010B/506